PATRICK H. PERRINE

Risk and Rally

Igniting Your Entrepreneurial Spirit in the High-Risk,
High-Reward Startup Journey

amazonkindle

DEDICATION

To the daring dreamers at the edge of the entrepreneurial frontier—this volume is for you. "Risk and Rally" is a beacon, illuminating the path through the tumultuous odyssey of startup ventures. It is dedicated to your unyielding spirit and unwavering resolve. Let this book serve as your armor and your guide, as you navigate the tempest of innovation and opportunity. Here's to transforming the daunting into the doable, the impossible into the inevitable.

Warmly,
Patrick

"Only those who will risk going too far can possibly find out how far one can go."

— T.S. Eliot

Contents

Preface

Embarking on the entrepreneurial journey is akin to navigating a complex dance of risk and reward, a theme we explored in Step 4 of 'Unicorn Rising.' In 'Risk and Rally: Igniting Your Entrepreneurial Spirit in the High-Risk, High-Reward Startup Journey,' we dive deeper into this intricate ballet, offering you a practical workbook that builds upon the foundational wisdom shared in 'Unicorn Rising.'

With two decades of entrepreneurship under my belt, this volume distills the essence of my experiences, focusing on the crucial ability to strategically navigate the interplay of risk and reward. 'Risk and Rally' serves not just as a narrative of my journey but as a guide designed to arm you with the tools, strategies, and mindset needed to thrive amidst the uncertainties of the startup world.

This book extends the exploration of risk and reward, introduced in 'Unicorn Rising,' by providing you with a detailed roadmap for understanding, evaluating, and strategically navigating these dynamics. Featuring practical exercises, actionable advice, and real-world case studies, 'Risk and Rally' is crafted to transition you from reader to doer, from dreamer to achiever.

As we journey together through the startup ecosystem, 'Risk and Rally' invites you to engage actively with the material. Exercises designed to apply directly to your ventures, case studies that illuminate the path walked by successful entrepreneurs, and strategies to balance risk and reward in your startup, are all aimed at empowering you to apply these lessons in real-time to your entrepreneurial endeavors.

This book is a testament to the belief that understanding the dance between risk and reward is at the heart of entrepreneurial success. It is your companion guide, offering a deeper dive into the concepts introduced in Step 4 of 'Unicorn Rising' and equipping you with the knowledge and tools to navigate the high-stakes journey of entrepreneurship.

Welcome to 'Risk and Rally.' Here's to embracing the calculated risks, celebrating the rewards, and igniting your entrepreneurial spirit as you chart your unique path in the high-risk, high-reward world of startups.

Be A Unicorn: The New Entrepreneur's Ultimate Guide To Success

Dream It, Build It:
An Aspirational Odyssey Through
Entrepreneurship in Ten Inspiring Volumes.

Volume Four

RISK AND RALLY

Igniting Your Entrepreneurial Spirit in the High-Risk,
High-Reward Startup Journey

1

The Startup Landscape

"Choose a job you love, and you will never have to work a day in your life."
— Confucius

Over the years, understanding the terrain you're traversing has proven to be the secret to effective navigation. In the entrepreneurial journey, this terrain is the startup landscape—an exhilarating yet intricate ecosystem. This chapter offers a panoramic view of today's startup landscape, marked by its complexities, opportunities, and the inevitable pitfalls, through the lens of recent entrepreneurial successes and the unique risks they've embraced.

The startup landscape, at its core, encompasses the entirety of entrepreneurial entities, ranging from modest solo ventures to towering tech unicorns. This ecosystem is not just about the startups but also involves investors, accelerators, incubators, regulatory frameworks, support services, and, crucially, the markets these startups aim to serve.

In an era of rapid evolution, traditional sectors like finance, healthcare, and education are undergoing significant upheavals, thanks to startups that leverage technology for innovative solutions. Concurrently, entirely new sectors have emerged, driven by advancements in technologies such as artificial intelligence, machine learning, blockchain, and virtual reality.

To bring clarity to this dynamic environment, we'll dive into the narratives of recent startups that have navigated these waters successfully, taking calculated risks along their path to achievement.

Opening Anecdote: NimbleRx: Revolutionizing Pharmacy Delivery

In the bustling world of health tech startups, NimbleRx has carved out a niche by revolutionizing the way prescriptions are delivered. Founded by Talha Sattar, NimbleRx partnered with local pharmacies to streamline the delivery process, ensuring medications reach patients quickly and efficiently. Sattar's vision was clear: to make prescription delivery as easy as ordering a book online. Despite the daunting challenges of navigating healthcare regulations and competing with giant pharmacy chains, NimbleRx's commitment to innovation and patient care has set a new standard in the industry.

Quick Thought:
Innovation thrives on understanding the ecosystem you're part of. The startup landscape, with its vast opportunities and inherent risks, is a testament to the entrepreneurial spirit's resilience and creativity.

Entrepreneurship in Action: Key Ingredients

- **Understanding the Ecosystem:** Grasping the complexities of the startup world is crucial. It's about recognizing the role of each player, from investors to regulatory bodies, and how they influence your journey.
- **Identifying Opportunities:** Successful entrepreneurs excel at spotting gaps in the market. They understand customer needs, sometimes even before the customers themselves do.
- **Risk Management:** The art of entrepreneurship is not just taking risks but managing them. Knowing when to pivot, when to persevere, and when to let go is essential.

Case Study: Pawame: Lighting Up Lives

Background: Alexandre Allegue embarked on a transformative journey with Pawame, aiming to electrify remote regions of Africa where conventional power remains a challenge. Recognizing the critical need for accessible electricity, Pawame introduced solar-powered solutions to light up homes and lives across the continent.

Innovative Financing for Accessibility: Central to Pawame's strategy is its pay-as-you-go model, a financial innovation making solar energy solutions affordable for households. This approach not only democratizes access to power but also introduces a sustainable model for energy consumption, reducing the initial financial barriers to renewable energy adoption.

Empowering Communities Beyond Illumination: The impact of Pawame's initiatives extends far beyond lighting.

By providing reliable energy sources, Pawame enhances educational opportunities through extended study hours, supports health by powering medical devices, and bolsters local economies by enabling longer business operations. This holistic approach to energy access fosters community development and uplifts entire regions from energy poverty.

Strategic Expansion Through Partnerships: Pawame's growth trajectory is marked by strategic alliances and a profound understanding of its consumer base. Collaborating with local organizations and leveraging insights into the unique needs of its markets, Pawame has significantly expanded its footprint, bringing light and hope to thousands of households across Africa.

Reflection: Pawame's journey under Alexandre Allegue's leadership is a testament to the transformative power of sustainable energy solutions in remote regions. By blending innovative financing with a commitment to community empowerment, Pawame lights the way for a brighter, more equitable future.

Case Study: Kiva: Empowering Entrepreneurs

Vision: Jessica Jackley co-founded Kiva with an inspiring mission—to forge connections across continents through lending, fostering poverty alleviation and entrepreneurial spirit. Kiva stands as a beacon of hope, linking lenders to entrepreneurs in distant corners of the globe, enabling dreams and driving economic empowerment.

Innovating Lending Through Technology: At Kiva's core is a revolutionary platform that transforms the traditional lending model. It allows individuals worldwide to contribute microloans to entrepreneurs, breaking down financial barriers and catalyzing small business growth. This platform embodies the digital age's power to unite people for a common cause, transcending geographical and cultural divides.

The Ripple Effect of Community Lending: Kiva's success story is written through the lives it has touched—millions of dollars in loans disbursed, countless dreams realized, and communities revitalized. This success underscores the profound impact of collective support and solidarity, illustrating how small acts of kindness can yield monumental change.

Charting New Horizons: With a forward-looking approach, Kiva continuously explores innovative pathways to expand its influence. From introducing new financial products to leveraging data for more impactful lending, Kiva is committed to evolving its platform to meet the dynamic needs of global entrepreneurs.

Reflection: Kiva's narrative, spearheaded by Jessica Jackley's visionary leadership, exemplifies the digital era's potential to bridge divides and nurture global communities. Through its pioneering platform, Kiva redefines philanthropy, proving that when humanity bands together, the possibilities for positive change are boundless.

```
Pro Tip: Remember, understanding the startup
landscape is not a one-time task. It's an ongoing
journey of learning, adapting, and evolving.
```

Exercise: Navigating the Ecosystem: Exploration, Assessment, and Engagement

Understanding the Startup Ecosystem

1. **Ecosystem Exploration Activity:** Identify and research five key components of the startup ecosystem (e.g., venture capitalists, accelerators, competition, customers, regulatory environment) in your sector. Create a detailed report on how each component influences startup success, including potential benefits and challenges.

2. **Trend Analysis and Forecasting:** Choose an emerging technology or trend within the startup landscape (e.g., blockchain, AI, remote work innovations). Analyze its current state, project its potential growth over the next five years, and explore how startups can leverage this trend for competitive advantage.

3. **Networking Strategy Development:** Develop a networking strategy aimed at integrating yourself or your startup more deeply into the startup ecosystem. Outline a plan for connecting with key players, including mentorship seeking, attending relevant events, and joining online communities. Set specific goals for each activity.

Risk Assessment

1. **SWOT Analysis for Your Startup Idea:** Conduct a SWOT analysis (Strengths, Weaknesses, Opportunities, Threats) for a hypothetical or real startup idea. Focus on internal factors (strengths and weaknesses) and external factors (opportunities and threats) within the startup

landscape.

2. **Regulatory Landscape Mapping:** Choose a sector and research the current regulatory landscape affecting startups in that area. Prepare a summary that includes potential regulatory hurdles, compliance strategies, and how changes in regulations could impact startup operations.

3. **Competitive Gap Analysis:** Perform a gap analysis by comparing your startup idea (or a hypothetical one) against the top three competitors in the market. Identify gaps in the market that your startup could fill, and propose a unique value proposition to address these gaps.

Strategic Action Planning

1. **Milestone Setting for Startup Development:** Outline the key milestones for the first two years of a startup journey, including product development, market entry, funding rounds, and scaling. For each milestone, specify objectives, expected outcomes, and key performance indicators (KPIs).

2. **Resource Allocation Plan:** Create a detailed resource allocation plan for a startup, considering financial, human, and technological resources. Include budgeting strategies, talent acquisition plans, and technology investment priorities to support startup growth.

3. **Customer Discovery and Validation Process:** Design a process for customer discovery and validation for a new product or service idea. Detail the steps for identifying target customers, collecting feedback, and iterating on the product based on user input. Include methods for both qualitative and quantitative feedback.

Challenge For You:

Select a sector within the startup landscape that intrigues you. Simulate a strategic planning session for launching a startup in this sector, addressing the ecosystem complexities, risk management, and your action plan for success. Create a comprehensive presentation or document outlining your strategy, incorporating the exercises above where relevant.

Conclusion

The journey through the startup landscape is fraught with challenges but also brimming with opportunities. As we've seen through the lens of startups like NimbleRx, Pawame, and Kiva, navigating this landscape requires a keen understanding of the ecosystem, an eye for opportunities, and a steadfast approach to risk management. The stories shared in this chapter are not just narratives of success; they're blueprints for aspiring entrepreneurs. They remind us that with the right mindset, every challenge is surmountable, and every risk, a stepping stone to success.

2

Understanding Risk

"The person who risks nothing does nothing, has nothing, is nothing, and becomes nothing. He may avoid suffering and sorrow, but he simply cannot learn and feel and change and grow and love and live."
— Leo F. Buscaglia

Following the exploration of the startup landscape, our voyage now delves into the essence of entrepreneurship's twin pillars: risk. The realm of startups is inherently fraught with risk; however, mastering the art of understanding and strategically managing these risks is pivotal for any entrepreneur aiming for success.

Risk, in its simplest form, embodies the potential for adverse outcomes, be it financial loss, tarnished reputation, or the collapse of the venture itself. But before we can effectively navigate these turbulent waters, a comprehensive understanding of risk—its nature, types, and our perception of it—is essential.

1. **The Nature of Risk:** Risk is an inescapable part of life,

inherent in every decision, from the mundane to the monumental. Yet, not all risks carry the same weight. While some are but pebbles on our path, others are boulders. In the entrepreneurial landscape, risks are magnified by the uncertainty shadowing every corner of the startup world. The acceptance and understanding of risk are thus foundational in steering through these uncertainties.

2. **Types of Risk:** Entrepreneurial risks are manifold, each with its own set of challenges and strategies for mitigation:

- **Market Risk:** The danger of a lukewarm market reception.
- **Financial Risk:** The hazards of financial instability.
- **Operational Risk:** Challenges in the day-to-day grind.
- **Regulatory Risk:** The threat of legislative shifts.
- **Technology Risk:** The peril of obsolescence or security breaches.
- **Team Risk:** The risk of internal discord or talent loss.

Grasping these risk types is the first step towards safeguarding your venture.

Risk Tolerance and Perception: Your risk tolerance—how much uncertainty you can stomach—and your perception of risk—how you view risk's severity—significantly influence your entrepreneurial journey. They dictate the risks you embrace and the ones you evade, shaping your venture's path.

Opening Anecdote: Fairphone: A Mission-Driven Risk

In the crowded smartphone market, Fairphone embarked on a bold mission to create ethical, durable, and repairable phones. Bas van Abel, Fairphone's founder, faced significant risks: competing against tech giants, convincing consumers to prioritize ethics over price or brand, and ensuring supply chain transparency. Despite these challenges, Fairphone's commitment to sustainability and fair labor practices not only distinguished it in the market but also ignited a conversation about ethical electronics, proving that mission-driven risks can lead to meaningful impact.

> *Quick Thought:*
> *Risk is the shadow and light of entrepreneurship; understanding it is not about avoidance but about strategic engagement.*

Entrepreneurship in Action: Key Ingredients

- **In-depth Market Analysis:** Vigilance in understanding market needs and trends can mitigate market risk.
- **Financial Prudence:** Careful financial planning and management are shields against financial instability.
- **Operational Agility:** Flexibility in operations allows for navigating unforeseen challenges.
- **Regulatory Compliance:** Staying informed on legal requirements can forestall regulatory surprises.
- **Tech Forwardness:** Investing in technology and cyberse-

curity fortifies against technological obsolescence.

- **Team Building:** Cultivating a strong, cohesive team is the best defense against internal risks.

Case Study: Chobani – Yogurt Revolution through Risk

Background: Embarking on an audacious journey, Hamdi Ulukaya ventured into uncharted territory by acquiring an old yogurt factory with the vision of creating Chobani. With limited experience in the yogurt industry, Ulukaya's leap of faith was not just a gamble; it was a bold statement on the power of innovation and quality.

Embracing Risk with Strategic Foresight: At the heart of Chobani's strategy was an unwavering commitment to quality, a distinct brand identity, and a pioneering approach to Greek yogurt. Ulukaya recognized the potential in a market that was ripe for disruption and steered Chobani with a clear focus on product excellence and brand differentiation. This strategic navigation of market risks set Chobani apart in a crowded industry.

Transformative Impact on the Market: Chobani's ascent to becoming a billion-dollar brand is a testament to the transformative impact of embracing and strategically managing risk. By redefining the dairy aisle in American supermarkets, Chobani did not just introduce a product; it created a cultural shift towards healthier, quality-focused food options. The brand's success propelled Greek yogurt to mainstream popularity, establishing Chobani as a household name.

Strategic Innovation as a Catalyst for Growth: Central to Chobani's narrative is the lesson that strategic risk-taking, coupled with a commitment to innovation and quality, can catalyze industry-wide revolution. Ulukaya's vision for Chobani hinged on the belief that consumers were ready for a change—a bet that paid off immensely.

Reflection: Chobani's journey from a risky start-up to a leading brand in the yogurt industry exemplifies how understanding and strategically managing risk can lead to groundbreaking success. Hamdi Ulukaya's gamble on an old factory was not merely a financial investment; it was an investment in a vision of changing consumer habits and making a lasting impact on the food industry. Chobani stands as a beacon for entrepreneurs that, with the right mix of risk, innovation, and strategy, revolutionary success is within reach.

Pro Tip: Engaging with risk is not a reckless plunge but a calculated dive. Knowledge, preparation, and adaptability are your lifelines.

Exercise: Balancing Act: Managing Sacrifice for Sustainable Success

Risk Exploration and Assessment

1. **Risk Identification Workshop:** Organize a workshop, either solo or with your team, to identify potential risks associated with your startup or business idea. Utilize a brainstorming technique to list as many risks as possible, categorizing them into market, financial, operational,

    regulatory, technology, and team risks.

2. **Risk Impact Scale Creation:** Develop an impact scale for assessing the potential severity of each identified risk. The scale should range from minimal to catastrophic, with criteria defined for each level. Apply this scale to the risks you've identified, ranking them according to their potential impact on your venture.

3. **Probability Assessment Exercise:** For each risk on your list, assign a probability of occurrence within a defined time frame (e.g., within the first year of operations). Use a simple scale such as high, medium, or low to quantify the likelihood of each risk materializing.

Strategic Risk Mitigation

1. **Mitigation Plan Development:** Select the top five risks based on their impact and probability ratings. For each, develop a detailed mitigation strategy that outlines specific actions, responsible individuals or teams, resources required, and timelines for implementation.

2. **Scenario Planning Session:** Conduct scenario planning for your top risks, imagining the best-case, worst-case, and most likely scenarios for each. Detail how your mitigation strategies would alter the course of these scenarios and plan for flexibility and adaptability in your responses.

3. **Preventative Measures Brainstorm:** Focus on preventative measures for each identified risk. Brainstorm innovative ways to prevent risks from occurring or reduce their impact through proactive steps. Consider technology solutions, process improvements, training programs, or changes in strategy.

Risk Perception and Tolerance

1. **Risk Tolerance Assessment:** Assess your own risk tolerance through a series of reflective questions or a formal assessment tool. Analyze how your risk perception might influence decision-making and identify areas where you could become more comfortable with taking calculated risks.

2. **Opportunity-Risk Reevaluation:** Choose a risk that you've identified as significant and reevaluate it as an opportunity. Brainstorm potential innovative solutions or business models that could turn this risk into a competitive advantage or new venture avenue.

3. **Feedback Loop Creation:** Design a system for regularly reviewing and updating your risk assessment and mitigation strategies. This should include scheduled reviews, criteria for revising risk priorities, and a mechanism for incorporating feedback from team members and stakeholders.

Challenge For You:

Pick one high-impact risk and initiate a project to transform it into an opportunity. Document your process, from the initial risk assessment through the development of a strategic plan, to the implementation of mitigation or transformation strategies. Share your findings and insights with peers or mentors for feedback and further refinement.

Conclusion

Understanding and managing risk is not about evasion but about strategic navigation. The journey through the world of startups is inherently risky, but it is these very risks that open the door to unprecedented opportunities. As we have seen with Fairphone and Chobani, approaching risk with knowledge, preparation, and adaptability can turn potential pitfalls into pathways to success. As we venture deeper into the intricacies of risk management in the chapters ahead, remember: the essence of entrepreneurship is not just to survive the storm but to dance in the rain.

3

Evaluating and Mitigating Risk

"Adaptability is not imitation.
It means power of resistance and assimilation."
— Mahatma Gandhi

With a solid grasp of risk's multifaceted nature under our belts, we pivot to a more hands-on approach: the dual processes of risk evaluation and mitigation. Mastery over these disciplines is indispensable for any entrepreneur aiming to navigate the tempestuous seas of startup life, where neglecting to properly assess and address risks can have dire consequences.

Risk Evaluation:
Embarking on the journey of risk evaluation, we confront two pivotal elements: the probability of a risk occurring and the potential impact of such an event. Estimating these aspects can feel like navigating through a fog for startups breaking new ground or pioneering innovative industries. Yet, armed with

data, market research, and informed forecasts, we can pierce through the uncertainty.

Risk Mitigation:

Having pinpointed our risks, we chart a course towards mitigation, wielding four primary strategies like a captain's tools for safe passage:

- **Risk Avoidance:** Altering course to steer clear of stormy waters.
- **Risk Reduction:** Fortifying the ship against the inevitable squalls.
- **Risk Transfer:** Enlisting a convoy to share the journey's perils.
- **Risk Acceptance:** Acknowledging the storm's presence, yet sailing on, prepared.

Opening Anecdote: Ecosia: Planting Seeds of Change Amidst Digital Giants

In the vast digital forest dominated by towering tech giants, Ecosia, a search engine with a mission to plant trees, took root. Founded by Christian Kroll, Ecosia faced daunting risks: competing against established search engines, convincing users to switch for an ethical cause, and ensuring the financial viability of its business model. Kroll's venture was not just about offering an alternative search engine; it was about integrating sustainability with everyday digital habits. Despite the odds, Ecosia's commitment to transparency, user privacy, and, most importantly, to reforestation has seen it plant millions of trees, turning the risky venture into a testament to the power of ethical entrepreneurship.

> **Quick Thought:**
> *Embracing risk is not a leap into darkness but a step into the light, illuminating paths to innovation and impact.*

Entrepreneurship in Action: Key Ingredients

- **Proactive Risk Analysis:** Keeping a keen eye on the horizon for emerging threats and opportunities.
- **Strategic Flexibility:** Navigating through risks with agility, adjusting sails as winds change direction.
- **Ethical Grounding:** Ensuring that every risk taken aligns with the venture's core values and mission.

Case Study: Beyond Meat – A New Frontier in Food

Background: Beyond Meat emerged on the culinary landscape with a bold mission: to redefine the future of food by offering plant-based alternatives to traditional animal protein. At a time when meat substitutes were a niche market, Beyond Meat took on the colossal challenge of convincing a global audience accustomed to animal-based diets.

Strategic Innovation and Market Entry: Beyond Meat's approach was multifaceted, focusing on relentless product innovation to mimic the taste, texture, and culinary experience of meat without the environmental and health downsides. Strategic partnerships with retailers, restaurants, and high-profile investors helped catapult the brand into the mainstream.

Aggressive and insightful marketing campaigns educated consumers on the benefits of plant-based eating, addressing preconceived notions and taste preferences head-on.

Navigating and Mitigating Risks: Beyond Meat tackled operational risks by scaling up production capabilities and supply chain logistics to meet growing demand. Market risks were mitigated through continuous product improvement and expansion into international markets, diversifying its consumer base. By listening to customer feedback and adapting quickly, Beyond Meat stayed ahead of emerging trends and competitive pressures.

Sustainable Success and Market Transformation: Beyond Meat's entry into mainstream markets has significantly shifted consumer perceptions of plant-based diets and highlighted the viability of sustainable food practices. The company's success story is not just about creating a popular product but about leading a global movement towards environmentally friendly eating habits.

Reflection: Beyond Meat's journey from a bold idea to a leader in the plant-based food industry illustrates the power of innovation, strategic risk management, and resilience in transforming challenges into opportunities. The company's success serves as a blueprint for entrepreneurs looking to make a significant impact, demonstrating that with the right approach, even the most daunting market and operational risks can be turned into avenues for triumph. Beyond Meat exemplifies how visionary thinking and a commitment to sustainability can alter industries and consumer habits worldwide, paving the way for a healthier, more sustainable future.

Pro Tip: The mastery of risk is not in its eradication but in the art of turning it to your advantage, crafting opportunities from challenges.

Exercise: Mastering the Risk Landscape: Evaluation, Mitigation, and Adaptation

Risk Evaluation

1. **Dynamic Risk Assessment Grid:** Construct a dynamic risk assessment grid for your startup or business idea. Populate the grid with risks identified across various aspects of your venture (market, financial, operational, etc.), assessing each risk for its probability of occurrence and potential impact. Use a color-coded system to visualize and prioritize risks.

2. **Trend Impact Analysis:** Conduct a trend impact analysis to understand how emerging trends in technology, economy, and society could influence the risks your startup might face. Write a brief report on potential shifts in risk profiles due to these trends and how your startup can adapt.

3. **Expert Insight Roundtable:** Organize a virtual or in-person roundtable with experts from your industry to discuss key risks and uncertainties within your sector. Prepare specific questions that seek insights on risk evaluation and how these risks have evolved. Summarize the findings and incorporate them into your risk management strategy.

Risk Mitigation

1. **Mitigation Strategy Playbook:** Develop a comprehensive mitigation strategy playbook tailored to the high-priority risks identified in your assessment grid. For each risk, outline specific mitigation actions, assign roles and responsibilities, and set timelines for implementation. Include contingency plans for different scenarios.

2. **Partnership and Collaboration Strategies:** Identify potential partnerships or collaborations that could help mitigate some of the risks your startup faces. Draft proposals outlining how these partnerships can work and the mutual benefits they offer, focusing on risk transfer and shared mitigation efforts.

3. **Innovation Lab for Risk Reduction:** Design an innovation lab session where you and your team brainstorm creative solutions to mitigate identified risks. Use design thinking principles to ideate, prototype, and test solutions that can reduce or eliminate risks. Document the process and outcomes for future reference.

Building Resilience and Leveraging Opportunities

1. **Resilience Training Workshop:** Organize a resilience training workshop for your team that focuses on emotional, financial, and operational resilience in the face of risks. Include exercises that enhance problem-solving skills, stress management, and adaptability.

2. **Opportunity Mapping from Risks:** For each major risk identified, conduct an opportunity mapping exercise. Look for hidden opportunities that each risk might

present, such as new markets, products, or innovations. Develop a mini business plan for one opportunity that shows promise.

3. **Learning from Failures Case Study:** Select a case study of a startup that failed due to one of the risks you've identified for your venture. Analyze the failure, focusing on what was overlooked in risk evaluation and mitigation. Prepare a presentation or report on the lessons learned and how they can be applied to your startup to avoid similar pitfalls.

Challenge For You:

Choose one significant risk from your assessment that poses a substantial threat to your startup. Use the exercises above to transform this risk into a growth opportunity for your venture. Document your strategy from evaluation to opportunity mapping, including the rationale behind your approach, the steps you will take, and the expected outcomes.

Conclusion: As we navigate through the world of startups, where risks lurk and opportunities abound, let us remember: the essence of entrepreneurship is not the evasion of risk but its astute management. The tales of Ecosia and Beyond Meat serve as beacons, guiding us through the uncertain waters with courage and conviction. In this chapter, we've armed ourselves with the knowledge and tools to evaluate and mitigate risks, embracing them not as foes but as catalysts for growth and innovation.

Forward we go, equipped with calculated courage, ready to turn the tides of risk into waves of opportunity. As we venture deeper into the entrepreneurial odyssey, let the mantra "The bigger the risk, the bigger the reward" fuel our aspirations, reminding us that in the daring lies the dream.

4

Cultivating a Culture of Risk Management

"Culture does not change because we desire to change it.
Culture changes when the organization is transformed; the
culture reflects the
realities of people working together every day."
— Frances Hesselbein

C ultivating a culture of risk management within a startup is not merely a strategic choice; it's a foundational shift that permeates every aspect of the organization. This cultural transformation is akin to constructing a resilient architecture capable of withstanding the unpredictable storms of the business world. In this chapter, we explore the intricate process of embedding risk management into the startup's DNA, ensuring it becomes a guiding force behind every innovation, decision, and growth strategy.

- **The Heartbeat of Innovation:** At the core of a startup's success is its ability to innovate while navigating the precarious landscape of risks. A well-integrated risk management culture serves as the heartbeat of this innovation, pumping wisdom and adaptability throughout the organization. It ensures that every leap towards innovation is measured, mitigated for risks, and aligned with the company's long-term vision.

- **Leadership as the Guiding Light:** The initiation and sustenance of this culture heavily rely on leadership's commitment. Leaders must not only preach the importance of risk management but also practice it, setting a precedent for the entire team. By embodying the principles of calculated risk-taking and transparent communication about potential pitfalls, leaders light the path for others to follow, instilling confidence and a sense of security amidst uncertainty.

- **Empowering Teams for Agile Navigation:** To maneuver through the volatile waters of the startup ecosystem, teams must be equipped with the necessary tools and knowledge. This empowerment enables them to identify risks proactively, assess them accurately, and devise innovative solutions. Education on risk management becomes a tool for empowerment, transforming potential hurdles into opportunities for growth and learning.

- **Fostering an Environment of Open Dialogue:** The culture of risk management thrives in an environment where communication flows freely. Open discussions about risks, failures, and the lessons learned from them encourage a collaborative approach to problem-solving. This collective intelligence strengthens the organization's resilience, making it more adept at predicting and responding to challenges.

- **Integrating Risk Awareness into the Fabric of Operations:** Celebrating risk awareness and seamlessly integrating risk management practices into daily operations are vital steps in making risk consciousness second nature to the startup. When risk management is embedded into the workflow, it becomes an intrinsic part of the decision-making process, ensuring that every action taken is a step towards sustainable growth.

Opening Anecdote: Glossier: Empowering Beauty Through Community-Centric Risk Management

Emily Weiss transformed a beauty blog into Glossier, a digital-first beauty brand that redefined industry standards by centering its strategy around consumer feedback and community. In the face of market saturation and shifting consumer trends, Weiss's approach to risk management involved closely listening to her audience to innovate products that genuinely resonated. This community-driven risk strategy not only fostered brand loyalty but also ensured Glossier's growth in a competitive landscape, showcasing the power of aligning business risks with customer needs.

> ### Quick Thought:
> *A culture of risk management is like the compass that navigates a ship through uncharted waters, ensuring that every member knows how to steer towards opportunity while avoiding the pitfalls.*

Entrepreneurship in Action: Key Ingredients

- **Leadership Commitment:** The cornerstone of a robust risk management culture is the unwavering commitment from the top. Leaders must not only advocate for but also embody the principles of risk awareness, setting a precedent that permeates through the organization.
- **Empowerment through Knowledge:** Equipping the team with the knowledge to identify, evaluate, and mitigate risks transforms passive participants into proactive guardians of the startup's vision. Education empowers each team member to contribute actively to the culture of risk management.
- **Open Communication:** Fostering an environment where discussions about risks are encouraged and valued ensures that potential threats and opportunities are identified and addressed collectively. Open communication is the lifeline that supports a culture of transparency and shared responsibility.

Case Study: Dropbox – Simplifying Technology in a Risk-Laden Landscape

Background: In its early days, Dropbox ventured into the cloud storage market, a domain rife with challenges ranging from intense competition to heightened security expectations. Founded by Drew Houston, Dropbox aimed to simplify digital storage, making it as seamless as using a physical hard drive but with the added complexities of online security and user accessibility.

Embedding Risk Management in Culture: Dropbox's strategy for navigating this complex landscape was to ingrain a culture of continuous risk assessment deeply into its operations.

This approach was pivotal in developing and implementing cutting-edge encryption technologies and advocating for robust user education on security practices. By prioritizing security and simplicity, Dropbox addressed the critical risks head-on, ensuring the platform remained both user-friendly and secure.

Securing Trust and Fostering Growth: The emphasis on a risk-informed culture has been instrumental in Dropbox's ascension as a leader in cloud storage solutions. The company's dedication to security and user experience has earned the trust of millions of users globally, facilitating its growth and solidifying its reputation in the market.

Insights into Cultivating Trust Through Risk Management: Dropbox's evolution highlights the significance of integrating risk management into the fabric of company culture. It demonstrates that addressing risks proactively, especially in industries where trust is paramount, can serve as a solid foundation for innovation, user loyalty, and sustained growth. Dropbox exemplifies that with the right approach to risk, challenges can be transformed into opportunities for building trust and driving technological advancement.

```
Pro Tip: The secret to cultivating a culture of risk
management lies in seeing risks not as threats but as
opportunities for growth and learning.
```

Exercise: Cultivating Resilience: Building a Risk-Aware Organizational Culture

Building a Risk-Aware Culture

1. **Culture Mapping Exercise:** Conduct a "culture mapping" exercise to identify current perceptions, practices, and attitudes towards risk within your organization. This involves creating a visual map that highlights how risk is currently identified, discussed, and managed at various levels of the organization, from entry-level positions to top management.

2. **Risk Management Principles Workshop:** Organize a workshop to develop a set of core risk management principles specific to your startup. This should be a collaborative effort involving team members from various departments. The goal is to create a unified set of values that guide your approach to risk, which will be integrated into your company's policies, training programs, and performance evaluations.

3. **Risk Communication Channels Audit:** Perform an audit of your current communication channels and protocols to evaluate their effectiveness in facilitating open discussions about risks. Identify any barriers to effective communication and brainstorm improvements. Consider establishing new forums or platforms dedicated to risk discussions, such as a monthly risk management meeting or an internal online forum where team members can report and discuss risks.

Leadership and Risk Management

1. **Leadership Risk Management Diary:** Encourage leaders within your organization to keep a "risk management diary" for a month, where they document the risks they encounter, decisions made in response to these risks, and the outcomes of those decisions. This exercise promotes reflection and learning from the risk management process, emphasizing the role of leadership in setting a risk-aware tone at the top.

2. **Risk Scenario Planning Session:** Facilitate a scenario planning session with your leadership team to explore potential future risks and how they could impact your organization. This exercise should include developing hypothetical risk scenarios and brainstorming strategic responses. The goal is to enhance strategic thinking around risk and improve preparedness for unforeseen challenges.

3. **Mentorship Program for Risk Management:** Establish a mentorship program focusing on risk management, pairing experienced leaders with less experienced team members. This program should aim to transfer knowledge about effective risk management practices and foster a culture where risk management is viewed as a shared responsibility.

Engaging Teams in Risk Management

1. **Risk Awareness Training Modules:** Develop and implement a series of training modules aimed at enhancing risk awareness among all team members. These modules

should cover topics such as identifying and assessing risks, developing mitigation strategies, and the importance of a risk-aware culture. Incorporate interactive elements such as quizzes, case studies, and simulations to engage participants.

2. **Team-Based Risk Mitigation Challenges:** Organize team-based challenges where groups are given a specific risk scenario related to their department or the organization as a whole and tasked with developing a mitigation plan. This exercise encourages teamwork, creative problem-solving, and practical application of risk management strategies.

3. **Feedback and Improvement Loop for Risk Management Practices:** Create a structured process for collecting feedback on risk management practices from team members across the organization. This could involve surveys, suggestion boxes, or dedicated discussion sessions. Use this feedback to identify areas for improvement and involve team members in the process of refining risk management approaches.

Challenge For You

Select one aspect of your organization's culture that poses a challenge to effective risk management (e.g., reluctance to discuss failures, siloed departments). Design and implement a targeted project to address this challenge, incorporating elements from the exercises above. Document the process, including any obstacles encountered and how they were overcome, as well as the project's impact on your organization's risk management culture.

Conclusion:

The journey to embedding a culture of risk management is both a challenge and an opportunity, requiring a steadfast commitment from leadership and active participation from every team member. It's a transformative process that not only prepares startups to navigate the uncertainties of the business world but also positions them to seize opportunities for innovation and growth. As we venture further into the exploration of risk and reward, let this chapter serve as a compass, guiding startups toward a future where risk management is not a hurdle but a stepping stone to achieving their loftiest ambitions.

5

Balancing Risk with Reward

"The biggest risk is not taking any risk... In a world that changes really quickly, the only strategy that is guaranteed to fail is not taking risks."
— Mark Zuckerberg

Navigating the delicate equilibrium between risk and reward is akin to an acrobat performing on a high wire, where precision, vision, and courage determine the success of the act. This chapter delves into this critical balance, essential for steering startups through the tempestuous seas of entrepreneurship to the shores of innovation and success. This segment aims to unravel the complexities of making calculated risks while safeguarding the startup's core values and long-term viability.

- **Strategic Equilibrium:** Achieving a harmonious balance between risk and reward is a strategic endeavor that requires careful analysis and foresight. Entrepreneurs must weigh the potential benefits of bold moves against the backdrop of inherent risks, ensuring that each calculated risk is a step towards fulfilling the startup's mission and enhancing its market position.

- **Navigating Uncertainties:** The journey involves navigating through uncertainties with a keen eye on both immediate opportunities and potential pitfalls. It's about making informed decisions that can propel the startup forward without jeopardizing its foundation. This strategic navigation is supported by a deep understanding of the startup's risk tolerance and an unwavering focus on its long-term goals.

- **Dynamic Adaptation:** The landscape of risk and reward is ever-changing, influenced by market trends, competitive dynamics, and internal growth. Startups must remain agile, ready to pivot their strategies in light of new information or shifts in the external environment. This dynamic approach to balancing risk with reward ensures that the startup remains resilient and responsive to opportunities for innovation and expansion.

- **Insightful Foresight:** At the heart of balancing risk with reward is the ability to anticipate future challenges and opportunities. Foresight allows entrepreneurs to prepare for various scenarios, making strategic adjustments to navigate their startup towards sustainable success. It's about seeing beyond the immediate horizon, planning for the long term, and steering the startup through uncharted waters with confidence and clarity.

- **Sustainable Growth Path:** The ultimate aim is to chart a course for sustainable growth, where risks are managed judiciously, and rewards are maximized. This path is paved with strategic decisions that align with the startup's values, market opportunities, and the evolving needs of its customers. Through this balanced approach, startups can achieve not just fleeting success but long-lasting impact and innovation.

Opening Anecdote: Oatly: Milking the Oat Market with Calculated Risks

Toni Petersson, CEO of Oatly, navigated the oat milk company through a landscape dominated by dairy and almond milk. By betting on the nascent oat milk market, Petersson's leadership involved taking calculated risks, from controversial marketing campaigns to aggressive expansion into new markets. Oatly's journey exemplifies balancing the risk of challenging conventional dairy norms with the reward of creating a new consumer trend, leading to a significant surge in demand for oat milk globally.

> ### Quick Thought:
> *Balancing risk with reward is akin to the art of surfing; it requires intuition, skill, and the courage to ride the waves of opportunity, all while navigating the undercurrents of uncertainty.*

Entrepreneurship in Action: Key Ingredients

- **Strategic Assessment:** The foundation of risk-reward balance lies in meticulously assessing both sides of the equation. This involves evaluating the market's potential, understanding competitive advantages, and discerning the financial and growth opportunities at play.

- **Dynamic Adaptability:** Entrepreneurs must cultivate the agility to adjust their strategies in real-time, responding to new information, market feedback, and internal progress with a flexible approach toward achieving their goals.

- **Informed Decision-Making:** At the heart of this balance is the capacity to make decisions grounded in robust analysis, foresight, and a clear understanding of one's risk tolerance. This strategic decision-making process ensures that risks are taken judiciously, with a keen eye on the potential rewards.

Case Study: Canva – Democratizing Design Through Calculated Risks

Background: Faced with the Herculean task of breaking into the design software market, Canva set out to democratize design, making it accessible to everyone from professionals to complete novices. This ambition placed Canva directly in competition with established giants like Adobe.

Strategic Risk-taking for User Growth: Canva's strategic gamble involved the introduction of a freemium model—a risky move intended to disrupt the traditional design software market. This model offered basic services for free while enticing users with advanced features through premium subscriptions. It was a calculated risk aimed at rapid user growth and market penetration.

Achieving Disruptive Success: Canva's risk was met with resounding success. The platform has become a go-to tool for millions, bridging the gap between professional designers and those without formal design training. Canva's intuitive interface and extensive template library have made high-quality design accessible to all, significantly expanding the market for design software.

Insights into Market Disruption: Canva's trajectory illuminates the critical balance between understanding market needs and boldly innovating to meet those needs. By offering unique value and simplifying the design process, Canva managed to not only enter but also thrive in a market dominated by long-standing players, demonstrating the power of strategic risk-taking in achieving scalability and impact.

Case Study: Slack – Redefining Workplace Communication

Background: Slack embarked on a mission to overhaul workplace communication, a domain crowded with traditional tools like email and proprietary instant messaging systems. This ambition to create a centralized platform for team collaboration presented significant risks, given the ingrained habits and existing solutions in organizations worldwide.

Innovative Approach to Market Entry: Slack's strategy revolved around leveraging its platform's integration capabilities and focusing on a user-friendly design that promised to streamline communication processes. The risk involved challenging established communication norms and convincing organizations to shift to a new, unproven platform.

Redefining Team Collaboration: The gamble paid off spectacularly, with Slack's platform quickly being embraced by startups, tech companies, and eventually a broader range of industries. Its success demonstrated the potential for innovative solutions to disrupt and redefine entrenched market norms, setting new standards for workplace efficiency and collaboration.

Balancing Innovation with Market Needs: Slack's ascendancy offers valuable lessons in balancing the risk of innovation against the reward of meeting and exceeding an unmet need in the market. Slack proved that with a clear understanding of user pain points and a commitment to addressing them through thoughtful innovation, it is possible to disrupt traditional spaces and foster a loyal user base.

```
Pro Tip: Mastery in balancing risk with reward comes
from not just taking risks, but taking smart
risks--those informed by data, grounded in reality,
and aligned with the strategic vision of the startup.
```

Exercise: The Tightrope Walk: Strategizing Risk for Maximum Reward

Strategic Risk-Reward Management

1. **Risk-Reward Analysis Exercise:** Create a comprehensive list of upcoming decisions or projects for your startup. For each item on the list, conduct a detailed risk-reward analysis. Use a structured framework to evaluate the potential benefits against the risks involved, considering both quantitative measures (e.g., potential ROI, cost) and qualitative factors (e.g., brand impact, strategic alignment). Summarize your findings in a decision matrix to guide your strategic planning.

2. **Dynamic Scenario Simulation:** Choose one high-risk, high-reward initiative from your analysis. Develop several dynamic scenarios for how this initiative might unfold, including best-case, worst-case, and most likely scenarios. For each scenario, outline strategic responses, contingency plans, and trigger points that would prompt you to reassess the situation. This exercise aims to prepare you for various outcomes and ensure that your startup remains agile and responsive.

3. **Innovative Risk Mitigation Workshop:** Organize a workshop with key stakeholders in your startup to brainstorm innovative risk mitigation strategies for the high-risk initiatives identified. Encourage creative thinking by exploring unconventional solutions, partnerships, and technology applications that could reduce risk without diluting potential rewards. Compile the most promising strategies into a risk management playbook for your startup.

Enhancing Risk Tolerance and Innovation

1. **Risk Tolerance Assessment and Expansion:** Assess your and your team's current risk tolerance through a series of reflective questions or assessments. Discuss the findings and identify areas where a higher risk tolerance could potentially unlock greater rewards. Develop a plan to gradually expand your risk tolerance through small, calculated risks that build confidence and resilience.

2. **Balanced Innovation Challenge:** Launch a challenge within your startup to propose new projects or initiatives that embody the perfect balance of risk and reward,

aligning with your strategic goals. Criteria for proposals should include a clear articulation of the risks involved, the potential rewards, and how the risk will be managed. Reward teams or individuals who present the most compelling and balanced proposals with the resources and support to implement their ideas.

3. **Risk-Reward Culture Embedding Activities:** Implement ongoing activities that embed a culture of balanced risk-taking within your startup. These could include regular 'failure forums' where teams share lessons learned from risks that didn't pan out, 'innovation sprints' focused on high-risk, high-reward projects, and recognition programs for team members who exemplify courage and smart risk-taking in their work.

Personal Development and Reflection

1. **Personal Risk-Reward Reflection Journal:** Keep a reflection journal over a period of one month, documenting decisions you face, the risks and rewards you perceive, and the outcomes of your decisions. Reflect on your decision-making process, how you managed the risks involved, and what you learned from each experience. Use this journal as a tool for personal growth in balancing risk with reward.

2. **Peer Learning Groups:** Form or join a peer learning group with other entrepreneurs or startup leaders focused on sharing experiences and strategies for balancing risk with reward. Use these groups as a platform to discuss challenges, share insights, and gain diverse perspectives on navigating the complexities of startup decision-making.

Challenge For You

Based on the exercises above, identify one strategic initiative that represents a calculated risk for your startup. Outline a comprehensive plan for launching this initiative, including risk assessment, mitigation strategies, expected rewards, and metrics for success. Commit to implementing this plan, monitoring progress, and adjusting as needed based on outcomes and learnings.

Conclusion:

The journey of entrepreneurship is punctuated with decisions that weigh risk against reward. Mastering the balance is not about avoiding risk but engaging with it thoughtfully, strategically, and with an eye towards the horizon of opportunity. As we continue to navigate the complexities of the startup landscape, let the insights from this chapter serve as your guide to making informed, bold decisions that propel your venture toward unprecedented heights of success and innovation.

6

Leveraging Risk for Growth

"The only way to discover the limits of the possible is to go beyond them into the impossible."
— Arthur C. Clarke

Embarking on the strategic pathway of leveraging risk for growth marks a pivotal chapter in the entrepreneurial journey. This chapter illuminates the art and science of transforming risks into catalysts for expansion, innovation, and market leadership. It's about navigating the intricate dance of taking bold steps forward while maintaining the agility to adapt and evolve. Here, we explore the foundations and strategies that empower startups to harness risks as drivers of transformative growth.

- **Embracing Leveraged Risk:** At the forefront of leveraging risk for growth is the acknowledgment that not all risks are to be avoided; some, when carefully selected and managed, can propel startups into realms of unexpected success. This realization encourages entrepreneurs to view risks not as mere obstacles but as opportunities ripe with potential for groundbreaking advancements.

- **Visionary Exploration of Opportunities:** The quest for growth is fueled by the ability to identify and seize opportunities that others might overlook. Whether it's breaking into untapped markets, launching innovative product lines, establishing strategic alliances, or pioneering new technologies, the ability to foresee and act upon these opportunities defines the entrepreneurial spirit.
- **Astute Evaluation:** Key to this strategic risk-taking is the rigorous evaluation of each opportunity, weighing potential benefits against associated risks. This meticulous analysis ensures that the pursuit of growth is grounded in realism and aligned with the startup's vision, capabilities, and strategic goals.
- **Methodical Risk Management:** This section delves into the tactical approaches to risk management, outlining how startups can embrace calculated risk-taking, diversify their growth initiatives, and implement effective risk mitigation strategies. These methodologies provide a framework for balancing the pursuit of growth with the imperative to safeguard the startup's core assets and future.
- **Adaptive Vigilance:** In the ever-evolving startup ecosystem, the ability to monitor, assess, and pivot is indispensable. Continuous monitoring of both external market dynamics and internal progress ensures that growth strategies are resilient, responsive, and attuned to the realities of the business landscape.

Opening Anecdote: Spotify: Harmonizing Risk and Innovation for Growth

Daniel Ek's Spotify journey illustrates the art of leveraging risk for growth. In its early days, Spotify faced the daunting challenge of negotiating rights with music labels and convincing users to pay for a subscription-based model in a market dominated by free downloading services. By embracing these risks and focusing on user experience and innovation, Spotify turned the tide, pioneering the music streaming service model. This strategic risk-taking not only propelled Spotify's growth but also transformed how the world accesses music.

> *Quick Thought:*
> *Leveraging risk in the startup ecosystem is akin to navigating uncharted territories with a compass of strategic foresight — it's about making informed moves that turn challenges into opportunities for growth.*

Entrepreneurship in Action: Key Ingredients

- **Visionary Leadership:** The impetus for leveraging risk for growth begins with leaders who dare to dream big and navigate the startup through the uncertainties of innovation and expansion.
- **Empowered Decision-Making:** Cultivating an environment where informed and agile decision-making thrives enables startups to seize opportunities with precision and adaptability.
- **Collaborative Synergy:** Harnessing the collective

strengths and insights of the team amplifies the startup's ability to identify, evaluate, and capitalize on growth opportunities through shared wisdom and diverse perspectives.

Case Study: Airbnb — Navigating Regulatory Risks for Global Expansion

Background: Airbnb, the trailblazer of the sharing economy, introduced a novel concept that redefined accommodation by tapping into the underutilized potential of private homes. This innovation, however, brought Airbnb into complex regulatory territories across different countries and cities.

Navigating the Regulatory Maze: The key to Airbnb's expansion lay in its adept navigation of the multifaceted regulatory challenges it encountered. Recognizing that each market's legal framework required a unique approach, Airbnb adopted a strategy of engagement, dialogue, and adaptation. By implementing comprehensive trust and safety measures, actively participating in community discussions, and tailoring its business model to align with local regulations, Airbnb turned potential roadblocks into opportunities for growth and advocacy.

Strategic Growth Through Collaboration: Airbnb's ability to engage with regulators and communities paved the way for its exponential growth. By transforming regulatory challenges into chances for partnership and policy advocacy, Airbnb not only expanded its global footprint but also championed the sharing economy model, establishing itself as a thought leader in the space.

Insights into Regulatory Adaptation: Airbnb's journey

underscores the significance of flexibility and proactive engagement in managing regulatory risks. It highlights how a thoughtful approach to navigating legal complexities can foster market expansion and enhance a company's reputation as an innovator and collaborator in the face of potential adversities.

Case Study: Stripe — Simplifying Global Payments with Technological Innovation

Background: Stripe entered the digital payments sphere with a mission to simplify online transactions for businesses and developers. In a sector dominated by established financial services and stringent regulations, Stripe's foray was marked by significant technological and security risks.

Embracing Technological Challenges: Stripe's strategy centered on leveraging cutting-edge technology to redefine payment processing. By focusing on developer-friendly APIs and prioritizing user experience, Stripe turned the technological challenges of the financial sector into a competitive edge. Its commitment to innovation was matched by an equally robust approach to security, ensuring that Stripe's platform remained resilient against cybersecurity threats.

Strategic Expansion and Security Focus: The calculated risks undertaken by Stripe in its pursuit of innovation and market expansion were instrumental in its ascent as a pivotal infrastructure provider for the digital economy. Through strategic global expansion and a relentless focus on enhancing security measures, Stripe not only navigated the complexities of financial regulations but also set new benchmarks for simplicity and reliability in online payments.

Leveraging Risk for Industry Leadership: Stripe's story

exemplifies how embracing and strategically managing technological and security risks can drive significant growth and sectoral transformation. Stripe's journey from a startup to a foundational component of the digital payments ecosystem demonstrates the transformative power of innovation, security, and strategic market engagement in leveraging risks for substantial growth and industry leadership.

> Pro Tip: The art of leveraging risk for growth lies in distinguishing between perilous gambles and strategic risks -- the former threatens stability, while the latter propels towards innovation and market leadership.

Exercise: Growth Through Uncertainty: Leveraging Risk Strategically

Opportunity Identification and Risk Evaluation

1. **Opportunity Scouting Exercise:** Conduct an opportunity scouting session to identify emerging trends, untapped markets, or innovative product ideas within your industry. Use tools like SWOT analysis (Strengths, Weaknesses, Opportunities, Threats) to uncover these opportunities and assess their alignment with your startup's strengths and market position.

2. **Risk-Opportunity Matrix Development:** Develop a Risk-Opportunity Matrix for categorizing identified opportunities based on their risk level and potential growth

impact. This matrix will help prioritize opportunities that offer the best balance between manageable risks and significant rewards. For each high-priority opportunity, outline the specific risks involved and the potential benefits.

3. **Dynamic Risk Assessment Workshop:** Organize a workshop with key team members to perform dynamic risk assessments on selected opportunities. Utilize scenario analysis to explore various outcomes based on different risk factors. This exercise encourages a deep dive into each opportunity's risk profile, fostering a comprehensive understanding and preparation for potential challenges.

Strategic Risk Leveraging and Mitigation

1. **Calculated Risk-Taking Plan:** Create a detailed plan for taking calculated risks associated with your prioritized opportunities. This plan should include clear objectives, risk mitigation strategies, implementation timelines, and key performance indicators (KPIs) for monitoring progress and impact.

2. **Innovation Sprint for Risk Opportunities:** Launch an innovation sprint focused on developing prototypes or pilot projects for exploiting the identified opportunities. This fast-paced, team-based approach encourages creativity and rapid problem-solving, allowing you to test ideas and assess their viability with minimal initial risk.

3. **Partnership and Collaboration Strategy:** Identify potential partnerships or collaborations that could mitigate risks while maximizing the opportunities for growth. Develop a strategy for engaging with these partners, outlining mutual benefits, roles, and expectations. This approach

leverages external expertise and resources, reducing the burden of risk on your startup alone.

Monitoring, Adaptation, and Learning

1. **Risk Monitoring Dashboard Creation:** Design a risk monitoring dashboard that tracks the progress of your strategic risk-taking initiatives against predefined KPIs. This tool should enable real-time monitoring of risk impact, providing data for informed decision-making and timely adjustments.

2. **Adaptive Strategy Review Sessions:** Schedule regular review sessions to assess the effectiveness of your risk leveraging strategies. These sessions should involve analyzing feedback, market responses, and performance data to identify necessary strategy pivots or enhancements, ensuring ongoing alignment with growth objectives.

3. **Post-Opportunity Reflection and Learning Document:** After executing a risk leveraging opportunity, document the process, outcomes, lessons learned, and areas for improvement. This reflective exercise promotes a culture of continuous learning and improvement, enhancing your startup's ability to leverage risk more effectively in future endeavors.

Challenge For You

Choose one opportunity with a favorable risk-reward profile from your exercises. Implement a comprehensive project to leverage this opportunity, applying the strategies and tools developed through the exercises. Document each step of the project, from planning and execution to monitoring and adaptation, including any pivots made in response to challenges or new information. Share your findings and insights with your team, fostering a culture of strategic risk-taking and continuous learning.

Conclusion:

Leveraging risk for growth is not merely about embracing uncertainty; it's about strategically navigating through it to unlock new dimensions of innovation and expansion. As startups journey through this landscape, the insights from this chapter serve as a compass, guiding towards a future where risk becomes the catalyst for groundbreaking success. Let the stories of Airbnb and Stripe inspire a bold approach to leveraging risk, transforming potential hurdles into monumental achievements.

7

Navigating Personal Sacrifice in Entrepreneurship

"The entrepreneur is essentially a visualizer and actualizer. He can visualize something, and when he visualizes it he sees exactly how to make it happen."
— Robert L. Schwartz

Setting out on the entrepreneurial journey is akin to setting sail on uncharted waters, where the thrill of discovery comes hand-in-hand with the necessity of personal sacrifice. This chapter delves into the deeply personal aspect of entrepreneurship, shedding light on the sacrifices that pave the path to innovation and success. Here, we navigate through the complexities of personal sacrifice, offering insights on achieving a harmonious balance between entrepreneurial ambitions and personal fulfillment.

- **The Spectrum of Sacrifice:** At the heart of the entrepreneurial experience is the understanding that sacrifices are not just a possibility but a certainty. These sacrifices span across time, dedicating countless hours to nurturing the business; financial resources, often investing personal savings into the venture; health, as the stress and demands of startup life take their toll; and relationships, which may strain under the weight of entrepreneurial commitments. Recognizing and accepting these sacrifices is the first step toward managing them effectively.

- **The Art of Balance:** Mastering the art of balance is critical in ensuring that these personal sacrifices do not overshadow the essence of living. It's about finding equilibrium where the pursuit of professional goals enriches rather than depletes one's personal life. This balance is dynamic, requiring constant attention and adjustment to align with evolving priorities and circumstances.

- **Making Strategic Sacrifices:** Not all sacrifices are created equal, and discerning which are necessary for growth— and how to undertake them—can set the foundation for both personal well-being and business success. Strategic sacrifices are those that propel the startup forward without compromising the entrepreneur's core values and health.

- **Cultivating Support Systems:** The journey is less daunting when shared with a strong support system of family, friends, mentors, and peers who understand and encourage the entrepreneurial endeavor. This network not only provides emotional sustenance but also practical advice and a safety net during challenging times.

- **Fostering Resilience and Recovery:** Building resilience, the ability to withstand and bounce back from adversity, is paramount. Alongside resilience, strategies for recovery— taking time to recharge, seeking professional help when needed, and engaging in activities that rejuvenate the spirit—ensure that entrepreneurs can sustain their efforts over the long haul.

Entrepreneurship demands a significant personal investment, but with careful navigation, strategic planning, and the cultivation of resilience and support, it is possible to traverse this landscape without losing sight of one's well-being and happiness. This chapter serves as a guide for entrepreneurs to make informed sacrifices, maintain balance, and ultimately thrive in both their personal and professional lives.

Opening Anecdote: Whitney Wolfe Herd: Bumble's Balanced Sprint

Whitney Wolfe Herd, the founder of Bumble, personifies the marathon of entrepreneurship and the personal sacrifices it entails. Wolfe Herd launched Bumble with a vision to empower women in the dating scene, a path fraught with personal and professional challenges. Her journey of balancing intense work hours with personal well-being mirrors the marathon runner's strategy—knowing when to push forward and when to conserve energy. Wolfe Herd's resilience and strategic pacing led to Bumble's success, proving the value of endurance tempered with self-care.

Quick Thought:
Personal sacrifice in entrepreneurship is not about how much you can endure but how you navigate these sacrifices to reach your goals without losing yourself in the process.

Entrepreneurship in Action: Key Ingredients

- **Strategic Time Management:** Prioritizing tasks and setting boundaries to balance work and personal life effectively. It's about working smarter, not harder.
- **Financial Wisdom:** Careful planning and management of personal and business finances to avoid overextension. Seeking external funding or investment can also alleviate personal financial pressure.
- **Health and Well-being:** Recognizing that personal health is the foundation upon which business success is built. Incorporating regular physical activity, mindfulness practices, and proper nutrition into daily routines is essential.

Case Study: Arianna Huffington's Thrive Global

Background: Arianna Huffington's journey to founding Thrive Global was sparked by a personal health crisis—a wake-up call stemming from sleep deprivation and exhaustion due to her relentless work ethic. This pivotal moment led her to champion the cause of well-being in the corporate world, transforming her personal sacrifices into a mission to redefine success.

Pioneering a Vision for Well-being: Thrive Global was born out of Huffington's newfound insight that well-being and productivity need not be at odds. By advocating for a holistic approach to professional life that includes mental health, mindfulness, and sleep, Huffington positioned Thrive Global at the forefront of a movement to integrate well-being into the corporate ethos.

Catalyzing Change Across Industries: Thrive Global's

impact has been profound and far-reaching, helping individuals and organizations worldwide recognize and implement practices that foster well-being alongside professional success. Through educational content, workshops, and corporate partnerships, Thrive Global has instilled a culture where balance is not only encouraged but also celebrated.

Lessons in Leadership and Innovation: Arianna Huffington's transition from media mogul to well-being advocate underscores the transformative potential of embracing personal challenges as catalysts for broader societal change. Her ability to turn personal sacrifice into a global initiative exemplifies how visionary leadership can inspire a shift in societal norms towards healthier, more sustainable modes of working and living.

Reflection: The story of Arianna Huffington and Thrive Global illustrates a critical lesson for entrepreneurs: personal well-being is an integral component of sustained success. Huffington's journey from collapse to global advocate for well-being challenges the conventional wisdom that sacrifice at the expense of health is a requisite for achievement. Instead, it presents a compelling case for the symbiosis between personal health and professional excellence, offering a blueprint for future leaders to thrive by prioritizing well-being as a foundation for success.

Pro Tip: Remember, enduring personal sacrifice is not a badge of honor but a signal to reassess and realign your priorities for sustainable success.

Exercise: Foundations of Endurance: Strategies for Sustained Growth

Personal Reflection and Strategic Planning

1. **Sacrifice Inventory Exercise:** Create an inventory of your current personal sacrifices in relation to your entrepreneurial journey. Categorize them into essential and non-essential sacrifices. Reflect on the impact of these sacrifices on your personal life and well-being, and consider which ones can be minimized or eliminated.

2. **Priority Alignment Session:** Conduct a session to align your daily activities with your long-term personal and professional priorities. Use a tool like the Eisenhower Box (urgent vs. important matrix) to organize tasks and identify areas where you can delegate, postpone, or eliminate activities that do not align with your core priorities.

3. **Boundary Setting Workshop:** Organize a workshop for yourself or with your team (if applicable) to establish clear personal and professional boundaries. Define specific times for work and relaxation, set communication guidelines, and commit to respecting these boundaries to ensure a healthier work-life balance.

Health and Well-being Integration

1. **Well-being Plan Development:** Develop a comprehensive well-being plan that includes regular physical activity, mental health practices (such as mindfulness or meditation), and nutrition. Schedule these activities into

your week as non-negotiable appointments to ensure they are prioritized.

2. **Stress Management Techniques Trial:** Identify and trial several stress management techniques over a month, such as deep breathing exercises, yoga, journaling, or speaking with a counselor. Evaluate their effectiveness in reducing stress and enhancing your overall well-being, adopting the most beneficial practices into your routine.

3. **Support Network Audit:** Evaluate your current support network, including family, friends, mentors, and professional peers. Identify gaps in support and take steps to strengthen your network through community engagement, professional associations, or by seeking out a mentor or coach who understands the entrepreneurial journey.

Resilience Building and Recovery

1. **Resilience Reflection Exercise:** Reflect on past challenges you've faced in your entrepreneurial journey. Identify the strategies that helped you overcome these obstacles and consider how they can be applied to future challenges. This reflection can help build resilience by recognizing your capacity to navigate adversity.

2. **Personal Recovery Plan:** Create a personal recovery plan for periods of intense work or stress. This plan should include activities that help you recharge, such as hobbies, time with loved ones, or short getaways. Recognize the signs of burnout and commit to implementing your recovery plan when these signs appear.

3. **Gratitude and Achievement Log:** Maintain a daily or

weekly log of achievements, moments of gratitude, and positive experiences. This practice helps shift focus from the sacrifices and challenges to the rewards and progress, fostering a positive mindset and emotional well-being.

Challenge For You

Choose one area of personal sacrifice that has significantly impacted your well-being. Implement a focused project to rebalance this area, incorporating the strategies and exercises outlined above. This could involve redesigning your work schedule, committing to a well-being activity, or enhancing your support network. Document the process, noting any changes in your stress levels, productivity, and overall happiness.

Conclusion

Navigating personal sacrifices in entrepreneurship demands a conscious effort to maintain balance, prioritize well-being, and harness support systems. It's about making strategic sacrifices without compromising the essence of who you are or your vision for the future. By adopting a balanced approach, entrepreneurs can journey through the challenges of startup life, not just to survive but to thrive, ensuring both personal fulfillment and business success.

8

Transforming Failures into Stepping Stones

"Success is not final, failure is not fatal:
It is the courage to continue that counts."
— Winston Churchill

The entrepreneurial odyssey is strewn with the debris of failures, each carrying lessons crucial for navigating the path to success. This chapter is dedicated to altering perceptions of failure, transforming it from a feared endpoint to a launchpad for growth and learning. Here, we delve into the transformative power of failure, emphasizing its role as a catalyst for innovation, resilience, and strategic evolution within the entrepreneurial landscape.

- **Embracing Failure as a Catalyst:** The first step in this transformative journey involves redefining failure. Rather than viewing it as a deterrent, successful entrepreneurs see failure as an inevitable stepping stone to greater achievements. This mindset shift is crucial for fostering resilience and encouraging a bold approach to innovation and risk-taking.

- **Strategic Learning from Failure:** Within each failure lies a wealth of insights waiting to be discovered. Entrepreneurs can employ techniques such as root cause analysis to dissect their experiences and extract valuable lessons. This process of reflection and learning ensures that every setback refines the approach and strategy for future endeavors.

- **Building Resilience Through Adversity:** The true mettle of an entrepreneur is often tested in the aftermath of failure. Building resilience— the capacity to recover quickly from difficulties— is pivotal. It's about developing the inner strength to persevere, adapting strategies in the face of challenges, and maintaining focus on the overarching vision.

- **Cultivating a Culture of Continuous Learning:** Transforming failures into stepping stones requires an organizational culture that values learning and adaptability. By encouraging open discussion of failures and the lessons they bring, entrepreneurs can foster a culture of innovation, where team members feel supported to take calculated risks and explore new ideas.

- **Implementing Actionable Transformation:** The ultimate goal of navigating through failure is to apply the lessons learned towards actionable change. Whether it's pivoting a product, adjusting a marketing strategy, or reevaluating a business model, the insights gained from past failures should inform and inspire future strategies and operations.

Opening Anecdote: Ringly: Smart Jewelry's Lessons in Market Timing

Christina Mercando d'Avignon, founder of Ringly, ventured into the uncharted territory of smart jewelry, merging fashion with technology. Despite Ringly's early lead in the wearable tech space, the startup faced challenges with market timing and consumer readiness. D'Avignon's journey, marked by pioneering innovation that was perhaps ahead of its time, underscores the importance of aligning product launches with market demands. Ringly's story serves as a lesson in transforming entrepreneurial vision into actionable insights for future endeavors.

> **Quick Thought:**
> *Viewing failure as a crucible for innovation transforms daunting challenges into valuable lessons, charting a course for growth and success.*

Entrepreneurship in Action: Key Ingredients

- **Constructive Analysis:** Delving into the 'why' behind failures, extracting actionable insights, and applying these lessons to future endeavors.
- **Open Feedback Loops:** Cultivating an environment where feedback is actively sought, shared, and valued, turning individual learnings into collective wisdom.
- **Celebration of Growth:** Shifting the focus from celebrating only successes to recognizing the growth and innovation spurred by overcoming challenges.

Case Study: Dyson — The Journey of 5,126 Failures

Background: Embarking on an ambitious endeavor to revolutionize the vacuum cleaner industry, James Dyson's journey was marked by relentless experimentation and resilience. The creation of the first bagless vacuum cleaner was not just an engineering challenge but a testament to the power of persistence, with Dyson navigating through 5,126 unsuccessful prototypes.

Embracing Failure as a Catalyst for Innovation: Each prototype, though not successful, served as a critical learning step for Dyson. These iterations were invaluable in deepening his understanding of airflow mechanics and dust separation technology. This iterative process underscored the importance of embracing failure as an integral part of the innovation journey, enabling Dyson to refine and perfect his design progressively.

Breakthrough Success and Industry Transformation: The persistence paid off with the success of the 5,127th prototype, marking the birth of the Dyson vacuum cleaner. This invention not only achieved commercial success but also set a new standard in the industry, challenging traditional notions of design and functionality in household appliances. Dyson's commitment to innovation and his refusal to settle for the status quo led to the creation of a product that stood out for its efficiency, design, and technology.

Insights into the Power of Perseverance: James Dyson's story is a powerful reminder that breakthrough innovations often emerge from the crucible of repeated failures. It illustrates how a steadfast commitment to a vision, coupled with the willingness to fail and learn from each setback, can drive extraordinary achievements. Dyson's journey from a series of failures to a revolutionary product highlights the transformative potential of viewing obstacles as opportunities for growth and learning.

Reflection: The narrative of Dyson's relentless pursuit of innovation through failure offers profound lessons for entrepreneurs and innovators alike. It exemplifies that the path to groundbreaking success is fraught with challenges and setbacks but that these can be surmounted with determination and a learning-oriented approach. Dyson's story encourages aspiring innovators to persevere in the face of adversity, reminding us that behind every success lies a journey marked by persistence, learning from failure, and the courage to continue pushing the boundaries.

```
Pro Tip: The essence of leveraging failure lies in
resilience -- the ability to face setbacks head-on,
extract wisdom, and forge ahead with an enhanced
blueprint for success.
```

Exercise: From Setbacks to Success: Learning and Evolving Through Failure

Reflective Analysis and Strategic Application

1. **Failure Audit Exercise:** Conduct a comprehensive audit of a recent failure, detailing what happened, why it happened, and how it affected your startup. Use tools like the Five Whys or SWOT analysis to dive deep into the root

causes and identify both internal and external factors that contributed to the failure.

2. **Learning Ledger:** Create a "Learning Ledger" to document the key insights gained from each failure. For every setback listed, record what was learned, how these lessons can be applied to improve future strategies, and any changes made as a result. This ledger will serve as a dynamic resource for growth and adaptation.

3. **Feedback Forum:** Organize a feedback forum with your team, mentors, or a peer network to discuss the failure openly. Present your analysis and insights from the Failure Audit Exercise and the Learning Ledger, and solicit additional perspectives. This collaborative approach can uncover blind spots and foster a culture of collective learning.

Building Resilience and Encouraging Innovation

1. **Resilience Workshop:** Facilitate a workshop focused on building resilience within yourself and your team. Include exercises on mindset shifting, stress management techniques, and storytelling sessions where team members can share personal experiences of overcoming adversity. This workshop can help normalize failure and emphasize its role in personal and professional growth.

2. **Innovation Challenge:** Launch an innovation challenge within your startup, encouraging team members to propose bold, experimental projects that address areas of previous failures. Provide a safe space for testing these ideas, with the understanding that failure is expected and valued as part of the learning process. This challenge can

spark creativity and lead to unexpected solutions.

3. **Pivot Planning Session:** Conduct a pivot planning session to explore strategic shifts or new directions in response to a significant failure. Use the insights gathered from your Failure Audit and Learning Ledger to guide discussions on potential pivots. This session should focus on how past failures can inform future strategies, emphasizing adaptability and strategic evolution.

Continuous Learning and Adaptation

1. **Post-Mortem Reviews:** Implement regular post-mortem reviews for projects or initiatives, focusing on those that did not meet expectations. These reviews should be conducted in a constructive manner, aiming to understand what happened, why it happened, and how similar outcomes can be prevented or improved upon in the future.

2. **Adaptation Roadmap:** Develop an Adaptation Roadmap outlining how the lessons learned from failures will be applied to current and future projects. This roadmap should include specific action items, responsible parties, and timelines for implementation, ensuring that the insights from failures are actively used to drive improvement.

3. **Personal Growth Plan:** Create a Personal Growth Plan focusing on areas of development identified through your experiences with failure. This plan should include goals for skill enhancement, mindset shifts, and strategies for managing adversity, with a focus on long-term personal and professional development.

Challenge For You

Identify a failure from your past that still impacts you or your business. Using the tools and strategies outlined in this chapter, reevaluate this failure to extract previously overlooked lessons. Develop and implement a plan to address the root causes of this failure, applying the insights gained to improve your business or personal approach. Document the process and outcomes, highlighting how re-engaging with past failures can lead to new paths of growth and success.

Conclusion

Failures, when approached with the right mindset, become stepping stones towards success. By embracing setbacks, extracting lessons, and persistently advancing towards your goals, you can transform the landscape of failure into a fertile ground for innovation and growth. This chapter not only aims to change how you perceive failure but also equips you with the strategies to navigate and leverage these experiences, ensuring your entrepreneurial journey is marked by continuous learning and enduring success.

9

Nurturing Long-Term Success

"Long-term success is the result not just of hard work and
dedication but also of the ability to adapt and grow amid the
ever-changing landscape of business."
— Indra Nooyi

As we journey beyond the initial triumphs and trials of entrepreneurship, the quest shifts towards cultivating enduring success. This chapter embarks on elucidating strategies to fortify and expand upon the hard-won achievements, ensuring the sustainability of your startup's success. The landscape of long-term success is complex, requiring a balanced approach to financial health, customer relationships, operational efficiency, continuous innovation, and employee engagement. Here, we explore the pillars essential for nurturing a startup's growth beyond its early victories, ensuring its legacy endures and flourishes.

- **Financial Prudence:** At the cornerstone of lasting success is financial stability. This section delves into the criticality of astute financial management, emphasizing strategies for maintaining healthy cash flows, prudent investment, and financial risk assessment. The goal is to build a financial buffer that not only shields the startup during downturns but also provides the flexibility to seize growth opportunities.

- **Customer Centricity:** The lifeblood of any startup is its customers. This part focuses on the importance of deepening customer engagement and loyalty. Through examples and strategies, it illustrates how understanding and anticipating customer needs, personalizing experiences, and building genuine relationships can turn customers into brand advocates, ensuring a stable and growing demand.
- **Operational Excellence:** Efficiency and agility in operations are pivotal for sustaining success. This segment discusses the significance of streamlining processes, leveraging technology for automation, and maintaining quality control. It showcases how operational excellence not only reduces costs and enhances productivity but also ensures the consistent delivery of value to customers.
- **Innovative Continuity:** In a rapidly changing market landscape, continuous innovation is key to staying relevant. Here, the focus is on fostering a culture of creativity, encouraging experimentation, and staying attuned to emerging trends and technologies. This approach ensures the startup remains at the forefront of industry evolution, meeting and shaping customer expectations.
- **Employee Engagement:** The final pillar of long-term success is the startup's team. This section underscores the importance of cultivating a motivated, skilled, and cohesive workforce. It explores strategies for employee

development, creating a positive work environment, and aligning individual goals with the company's vision. Engaged employees are not just more productive; they are instrumental in driving innovation and embodying the startup's values.

Opening Anecdote: Calendly: Scheduling Success Through User-Centric Growth

Tope Awotona poured his savings into creating Calendly, a scheduling software aimed at simplifying meeting coordination. Focusing on user experience and seamless integration, Awotona's dedication to solving a common problem paid off, with Calendly becoming an indispensable tool for professionals worldwide. Calendly's growth, fueled by a relentless focus on customer feedback and continuous improvement, highlights how nurturing a startup involves prioritizing long-term user satisfaction over short-term gains.

> ### Quick Thought:
> *Sustaining success in entrepreneurship is akin to gardening through the seasons; it demands foresight, care, and the willingness to adapt to ensure continuous growth and beauty.*

Entrepreneurship in Action: Key Ingredients

- **Strategic Financial Management:** Adopting practices for robust financial health, including revenue diversification, cost management, and investment in growth opportunities.

- **Customer Engagement and Loyalty:** Implementing strategies to deepen customer relationships through exceptional service, personalized experiences, and active engagement initiatives.
- **Embracing Technological Advancements:** Leveraging technology to streamline operations, innovate product offerings, and enhance customer interactions, ensuring operational agility and competitiveness.

Case Study: Patagonia — Commitment to Sustainability and Quality

Background: Patagonia's ascent to the pinnacle of the outdoor apparel industry is a narrative of deep-rooted values and unwavering commitment to environmental sustainability and product quality. This commitment has not only defined Patagonia's operational ethos but has also endeared it to a global community of environmentally conscious consumers.

Cultivating a Community of Advocacy: Central to Patagonia's sustained success is its ability to engage and nurture a community around its core values. The "Worn Wear" program exemplifies this, encouraging customers to repair, share, and recycle their gear, thereby extending the lifecycle of products and reducing environmental impact. This initiative strengthens Patagonia's brand identity and fosters deep, lasting customer loyalty, creating a network of advocates for both the brand and its environmental mission.

Leadership in Sustainable Innovation: Patagonia's investment in innovation extends beyond product design to embrace sustainable materials and eco-friendly production methods. This commitment to sustainability is evident in its supply chain choices, from sourcing organic cotton to pioneering the use of recycled materials and renewable energy in manufacturing processes. By prioritizing sustainability as a core aspect of innovation, Patagonia not only leads by example but also challenges industry norms and inspires change.

Setting a New Industry Paradigm: The influence of Patagonia's sustainability-first approach has reverberated across the apparel industry and beyond, prompting competitors and consumers alike to reconsider their environmental impact. Patagonia's dedication to its values has not only set new standards for corporate responsibility but has also demonstrated the feasibility of aligning business success with environmental stewardship.

Reflection: Patagonia's journey underscores the profound impact of integrating core values with business strategy to nurture long-term success. The company's story is a testament to the power of building a brand around sustainability, community engagement, and continuous innovation. It serves as an inspiring example for businesses aiming to achieve commercial success without compromising on their commitment to societal and environmental values. Patagonia stands as a beacon for entrepreneurs and business leaders, illustrating that long-term success is not only measured by profit margins but also by the positive impact on the world and the legacy left for future generations.

Pro Tip: The key to nurturing long-term success lies in the delicate balance between steadfastness to core values and agility in adapting to new challenges and opportunities.

Exercise: Shaping Your Entrepreneurial Destiny

Financial Stability and Growth

1. **Comprehensive Financial Review:** Conduct a thorough review of your startup's financial status, including cash flow, revenue streams, expenses, and investments. Identify areas for optimization, such as reducing unnecessary expenses, diversifying income sources, or reallocating resources for better returns. Develop a plan to address these areas, setting clear objectives and timelines.

2. **Risk Assessment and Contingency Planning:** Perform a risk assessment focusing on financial vulnerabilities, such as dependency on a limited number of clients, market fluctuations, or regulatory changes. For each identified risk, create a contingency plan that outlines strategies to mitigate impact, ensuring your startup remains financially resilient.

Customer Engagement and Loyalty

1. **Customer Journey Mapping:** Map out the customer journey from discovery through to purchase and beyond. Identify key touchpoints and assess whether they effectively engage customers and meet their needs. Based on this analysis, pinpoint opportunities to enhance the customer experience, personalization, and follow-up, aiming to increase satisfaction and loyalty.

2. **Feedback Loop Enhancement:** Evaluate your current mechanisms for gathering and responding to customer feedback. Develop a plan to strengthen these feedback

loops, incorporating regular surveys, focus groups, or one-on-one interviews. Ensure there are clear processes for acting on feedback, demonstrating to customers that their input is valued and leads to tangible improvements.

Operational Efficiency and Innovation

1. **Operational Process Audit:** Audit your startup's operational processes to identify inefficiencies, bottlenecks, or areas where technology could automate repetitive tasks. Select one or two key processes for optimization, and implement solutions designed to streamline operations, improve productivity, and reduce costs.

2. **Innovation Workshop:** Host an innovation workshop with your team to brainstorm new ideas for products, services, or business models. Encourage thinking beyond current market offerings, focusing on emerging trends, technologies, and unmet customer needs. Prioritize ideas based on their potential impact and alignment with your startup's goals, and outline steps for prototyping the most promising concepts.

Cultivating a Motivated and Cohesive Team

1. **Employee Engagement Survey:** Conduct an anonymous employee engagement survey to gauge team satisfaction, morale, and areas for improvement. Use the insights gained to address concerns, enhance work conditions, and foster a positive, supportive culture that aligns with your startup's values and objectives.

2. **Professional Development Planning:** Work with each

team member to develop a personalized professional development plan that aligns with their career goals and the startup's needs. Incorporate opportunities for skill enhancement, leadership training, and cross-functional projects designed to promote growth, satisfaction, and retention.

Challenge For You

Select one of the exercises above that you believe will have the most significant impact on your startup's long-term success. Implement the exercise, documenting the process, outcomes, and any adjustments made along the way. Reflect on how this initiative has strengthened your startup's foundation for sustainable growth and plan additional actions based on your learnings.

Conclusion

Nurturing long-term success transcends mere survival; it's about thriving in an ever-evolving landscape through strategic foresight, financial wisdom, and a commitment to innovation and community. As we close this chapter, remember that the journey of entrepreneurship is a marathon, not a sprint. By adopting the strategies outlined herein, you position your startup not just to succeed today but to flourish for years to come, leaving a lasting impact on your industry and community.

10

The Entrepreneur's Journey – A Retrospective and Looking Ahead

"The entrepreneur is essentially a visualizer and actualizer... He can visualize something, and when he visualizes it he sees exactly how to make it happen."
— *Robert L. Schwartz*

Positioned at the brink of concluding our exploration into the entrepreneurial journey, it's crucial to reflect on the paths traversed and to chart the course ahead.This chapter serves as a beacon, guiding through introspection and forward-thinking, preparing you for the continuous adventure of entrepreneurship.

Embarking on a retrospective journey illuminates the growth, achievements, challenges, and invaluable lessons encountered. It's crucial to:

- **Reflect on Growth:** Consider how you've evolved, the skills acquired, and the wisdom garnered.

- **Acknowledge Achievements:** Recognize the milestones reached and their impact on your venture and community.
- **Learn from Challenges:** Embrace the hurdles overcome, analyzing them as crucial learning moments that have fortified your resolve and acumen.
- **Distill Learnings:** Pinpoint the key insights from both successes and failures, allowing them to inform future strategies.

Looking Ahead – Charting the Future Course:

Armed with reflections, setting sights on the horizon involves:

- **Goal Setting:** Establish clear, actionable objectives that resonate with your vision, serving as your compass.
- **Strategic Planning:** Craft detailed plans encompassing actions, resources, and timelines, laying a roadmap towards achieving these goals.
- **Continuous Learning:** Identify areas for growth, embracing knowledge and experiences that will augment your entrepreneurial toolkit.
- **Proactive Risk Management:** Foresee potential challenges, devising strategies to mitigate them, safeguarding your venture's journey ahead.

The Entrepreneur's Mindset:

The essence of sustained entrepreneurial success lies in nurturing a conducive mindset:

- **Growth Mindset:** Embrace continual learning and improvement, viewing challenges as opportunities to evolve.

- **Resilience:** Develop the fortitude to weather setbacks, using them as stepping stones rather than roadblocks.
- **Innovation:** Keep the flame of innovation alive, staying adaptable and responsive to the ever-changing business landscape.
- **Leadership:** Cultivate leadership that inspires, motivates, and drives your team towards collective success.

Opening Anecdote: Reid Hoffman and LinkedIn: Connecting Past Success with Future Vision

Reid Hoffman's journey with LinkedIn showcases the essence of looking back to move forward. As one of the co-founders, Hoffman leveraged his experiences and lessons from previous ventures to guide LinkedIn's strategy, focusing on creating a platform that would redefine professional networking. By reflecting on past challenges and successes, Hoffman and his team built LinkedIn into a global network, continuously adapting and innovating to meet the future head-on. This story highlights the importance of retrospection in paving the way for future advancements and achievements.

> *Quick Thought:*
> *Entrepreneurship is an ever-evolving journey that demands not just a reflection on the past but also a visionary outlook towards the future.*

Entrepreneurship in Action: Key Ingredients

- **Reflective Practice:** Regularly taking stock of achievements, challenges overcome, and lessons learned, using these insights to refine strategies and approaches.

- **Strategic Goal Setting:** Identifying new objectives based on past performance and future aspirations, setting a roadmap for continued growth and innovation.
- **Adaptive Planning:** Being prepared to pivot and adapt strategies in response to emerging trends, market demands, and internal growth.

Case Study: SpaceX — Reaching for the Stars with Visionary Goals

Background: SpaceX's transformative journey from its precarious early days to becoming a titan of space exploration is a tale of vision, resilience, and groundbreaking achievements. Spearheaded by Elon Musk, SpaceX overcame near bankruptcy and a series of failed launches to position itself at the forefront of the aerospace industry.

Revolutionizing Space Travel: SpaceX's commitment to reducing space travel costs and its ambition for Mars colonization have catalyzed significant advancements in space technology. The development and successful landing of reusable rockets represent a pivotal innovation, drastically reducing the cost of space exploration and making the dream of Mars colonization more tangible.

The Power of Visionary Leadership: Central to SpaceX's success is Elon Musk's unwavering vision and his relentless pursuit of seemingly impossible goals. Musk's leadership has not only propelled SpaceX to achieve historic milestones, such as the first privately funded spacecraft to reach the International Space Station but has also ignited a renewed global interest in space exploration.

Reflection: SpaceX's journey underscores the essence of entrepreneurial spirit—transforming vision into reality through perseverance, innovation, and a bold willingness to challenge the status quo. It exemplifies how visionary leadership and a commitment to long-term goals can lead to revolutionary breakthroughs that redefine industries and expand human potential.

```
Pro Tip: Cultivate the habit of looking back only to
learn and forge ahead with greater wisdom, clarity,
and determination.
```

Exercise: Charting the Course: Reflect, Plan, and Evolve:

Reflecting on the Past

1. **Journey Mapping:** Create a visual timeline of your entrepreneurial journey thus far. Mark significant milestones, key challenges, and pivotal moments of learning. Reflect on each phase, noting how it shaped your business and personal growth.

2. **Lessons Learned Ledger:** Compile a ledger of the most critical lessons learned throughout your entrepreneurial journey. For each lesson, write down a situation that taught you this lesson and how it has influenced your decision-making processes or business strategies.

3. **Gratitude and Growth Reflection:** Write a reflective

piece expressing gratitude towards the experiences, people, and even the setbacks you've encountered. Highlight how these elements have contributed to your growth, emphasizing the value of each in your entrepreneurial evolution.

Planning for the Future

1. **Visionary Goal Setting:** Identify and articulate at least three visionary goals for the future of your startup. These should be ambitious yet achievable goals that stretch your capabilities and drive your venture forward.
2. **Strategic Roadmap Development:** For each visionary goal identified, develop a strategic roadmap outlining the key actions, milestones, and timelines necessary to achieve these objectives. Include resources needed and potential obstacles, with strategies to overcome them.
3. **Continuous Learning Plan:** Draft a continuous learning plan for yourself and your team. Identify areas where new skills or knowledge are required to achieve your future goals. Outline steps for acquiring this expertise, such as workshops, courses, or mentorship programs.

Cultivating the Entrepreneurial Mindset

1. **Growth Mindset Workshop:** Conduct a workshop for yourself and your team focused on fostering a growth mindset. Include exercises to challenge fixed mindset attitudes, celebrate efforts and learning from mistakes, and encourage adaptability.
2. **Resilience Building Activities:** Design a set of activities

aimed at building resilience, both personally and within your team. These could include scenario planning for setbacks, resilience storytelling sessions, or team-building challenges that simulate and navigate through potential business adversities.

3. **Innovation Incubation Sessions:** Schedule regular innovation incubation sessions where team members can pitch new ideas, no matter how bold or unconventional. Establish a supportive environment for evaluating these ideas, focusing on potential rather than immediate practicality, to encourage continuous innovation and adaptability.

Challenge For You

Choose one of the visionary goals you've set and initiate a project or initiative aimed at bringing you closer to this goal. Apply the lessons learned from your past and the strategies developed for the future. Document the process, including any pivots or adaptations, and analyze the outcomes, focusing on growth and learning over immediate success.

Conclusion: Embracing the Journey Ahead:

The journey of entrepreneurship is a continuum of learning, growth, and reinvention. As this chapter closes, let the stories from this book inspire you to dream bigger, act bolder, and forge a path marked by resilience and innovation. Remember, entrepreneurship is more than reaching destinations; it's about the richness of the journey, the learning in the process, and the impact you create.

The road ahead is replete with possibilities waiting to be discovered. With the insights and strategies shared throughout this guide, you are equipped to navigate the future with confidence, creativity, and a commitment to making a difference. Here's to your entrepreneurial journey and the endless horizons that await exploration.

Epilogue: Charting Uncharted Waters in the Entrepreneurial Odyssey

As "Risk and Rally" comes to a close, we find ourselves at the cusp of new beginnings, standing on the precipice of untold stories of entrepreneurship yet to unfold. Through the pages of this guide, we've navigated the intricate dance of risk and reward, journeyed through the trials of personal sacrifice, and celebrated the resilience born from failures transformed into stepping stones. Now, it's time to cast our gaze forward, drawing upon the essence of our shared odyssey to ignite the entrepreneurial spirit that lies within each of us.

Recap of Key Insights and Strategies: "Risk and Rally" was conceived as a lantern in the dense fog of entrepreneurship, illuminating paths less traveled and revealing strategies to harness the tumultuous seas of startup ventures. We've delved into the foundational principles of risk management, the alchemy of transforming risk into growth, and the artistry behind sustaining long-term success. Each chapter was meticulously crafted to arm you with the tools necessary to navigate the high-stakes environment of entrepreneurship, from the initial spark of an idea to the enduring legacy of a successful venture.

The Entrepreneur's Compass: Continuous Learning and Evolution: The journey of entrepreneurship is perpetual, marked not by destinations but by continuous evolution. It beckons you to remain a lifelong student of the ever-changing business landscape, to adapt, to pivot, and to embrace the unknown with curiosity and courage. Let the insights from "Risk and Rally" serve as your compass, guiding you through future ventures with an unwavering commitment to growth, innovation, and resilience.

Empowering Future Entrepreneurs: A Call to Action: As you step into the next chapter of your entrepreneurial journey, remember that your experiences, both triumphs, and trials, are invaluable lessons not just for you but for the broader entrepreneurial community. I invite you to share your story, to mentor aspiring entrepreneurs, and to contribute to a vibrant ecosystem where ideas flourish, risks are celebrated, and failures are viewed as precious learning opportunities.

Embracing the Unknown with Optimism and Purpose: The path ahead is uncharted, filled with potential risks and boundless rewards. It is a testament to the entrepreneurial spirit to venture into these unknown waters with optimism, guided by the principles of strategic risk-taking, personal resilience, and a deep-seated purpose. Your journey is a beacon of inspiration, a testament to the courage and determination that define the heart of an entrepreneur.

Conclusion: A Beacon for Future Ventures: "Risk and Rally" was penned with the hope that it would be more than a guide—it was envisioned as a companion on your entrepreneurial journey, a source of inspiration and wisdom for the challenges and opportunities that lie ahead. As we part ways, may the spirit of entrepreneurship burn ever brighter within you, propelling you towards horizons yet unseen, towards ventures bold and new.

With gratitude and best wishes, I bid you farewell on this leg of your journey, knowing that the true adventure lies in the paths you choose to forge from here. May "Risk and Rally" be a beacon that lights your way, and may your entrepreneurial journey be marked by relentless pursuit, indomitable spirit, and, above all, the courage to rally in the face of risk.

Until our paths cross again, keep rallying.

The Ask

Dear Visionary Explorer,

As we conclude our journey through the high-stakes world of entrepreneurship in "Risk and Rally," I hope it has empowered you, sparked insight, and equipped you for the thrilling path ahead. If this guide has been a compass in navigating the unpredictable terrains of startup success and challenges, I warmly invite you to share your experience by leaving a review on Amazon.

Your insights are invaluable, not only to me as an author but to fellow and future entrepreneurs embarking on their own ventures. Whether this book has served as a guiding light, sparked a moment of revelation, or you see room for refinement, your feedback contributes to the collective wisdom that supports the entrepreneurial community.

For those eager to delve deeper into the odyssey of entrepreneurship, I encourage you to visit my Amazon author page (https://www.amazon.com/author/patrickhperrine) where the exploration into innovation, risk, and reward continues.

Together, let's inspire and nurture the spirit of entrepreneurship, sharing our learnings and lifting each other up, one insightful review at a time.

With Gratitude and Solidarity,
Patrick H. Perrine

About the Author

Patrick H. Perrine is a trailblazing author, mentor, and seasoned entrepreneur with a spirit that exemplifies the essence of entrepreneurship. From his humble beginnings as a paperboy in Minnesota to his emergence as a globally recognized industry leader, his journey epitomizes resilience and determination.

Fueled by an insatiable thirst for knowledge, Patrick opted for university over his senior high school year, setting the stage for his relentless pursuit of personal growth. His tenure with UpStart, an organization championing educational opportunities for first-generation Americans, ignited his lifelong commitment to empowering others, extending beyond business and into his early philanthropic endeavors.

In his twenties, Patrick served as a Founding Board member for The Point Foundation, the largest LGBTQ scholarship foundation today. His dedication to fostering inclusivity and aiding LGBTQ students in higher education continues to positively impact hundreds of lives.

Patrick's entrepreneurial journey took flight with myPartner.com, an online dating service that addressed a critical gap in the market. Recognized as one of the "Best Matchmakers" and "Most Innovative Online Dating Sites" by the iDate Industry, the venture earned a Certificate of Recognition issued by California Legislature Assemblyman Mark Leno. This marked Patrick's first step in a journey filled with identifying unique opportunities and delivering transformative solutions across industries from skincare to dog tech.

Despite the hurdles encountered, Patrick's determination only amplified. His passion for nurturing startups led him to establish Rincon Hill Advisors. During this period, he served as a Steering Committee member for StartOut, a leading nonprofit fostering queer entrepreneurship, and consulted with Fortune 500 companies like Berkshire Hathaway and Intuit.

Adding to his achievements as an entrepreneur, Patrick became an angel investor. His foresight led him to invest in promising startups like MisterB&B, the world's largest gay hotelier, and Roadster, the leading commerce platform for car buying. His dog tech venture, too, gained recognition, leading to his selection as a NGLCC Pitch Finalist and participant in the Seamless IoT Accelerator, earning a $100,000 investment offer as a program graduate.

Most recently, Patrick served as an Entrepreneur in Residence (EiR) with 500 StartUps, an organization committed to uplifting global economies through entrepreneurship. This role solidified his dedication to guiding and uplifting aspiring entrepreneurs.

With multiple books to his credit, including recent works "Fail Fast, Recover Faster", "Ignite Your Dream", and "Fueling the Fire," Patrick continues to share his journey and insights. His writing reflects his unwavering commitment to guiding entrepreneurs through their unique journeys.

Patrick H. Perrine is more than a summary of his accomplishments. He stands as a testament to the power of determination, innovation, and a generous spirit. His contributions have been acknowledged in global press publications such as Forbes, Advocate, and Mirror, but his most profound impact lies in the lives of the entrepreneurs he's guided, inspired, and empowered. As he continues sharing his wisdom in the 10 volume series "Be A Unicorn: The New Entrepreneur's Ultimate Guide to Success," Patrick personifies the quintessential entrepreneurial journey—one of resilience, innovation, and the relentless pursuit of personal growth.

Subscribe to my newsletter:

✉ https://patrickperrine.com

Also by Patrick H. Perrine

Your next adventure in entrepreneurship awaits! Choose your guidebook on Amazon (https://www.amazon.com/author/patrickhperrine) or **www.PatrickPerrine.com**, and ignite the spark that takes your venture to new heights. The future is yours to shape!

Unicorn Rising: Ascending to the Pinnacle of Entrepreneurship and the Billionaire's Club

Fueled by entrepreneurial dreams and the allure of the Unicorn Club? Patrick H. Perrine is your guide, offering an unparalleled roadmap set to be every entrepreneur's playbook.

"Unicorn Rising" emerges as the cornerstone of the *Be A Unicorn* series, laying the groundwork that "Risk and Rally" and the other nine volumes build upon.

This seminal work provides an in-depth exploration into the entrepreneurial journey, offering a comprehensive roadmap for those aiming to scale their ventures to the heights of the Unicorn Club.

Driven by the dream of entrepreneurial excellence and a place in the Unicorn Club? Patrick H. Perrine offers an unmatched guide, positioning this book as the ultimate playbook for entrepreneurs.

Within "Unicorn Rising," readers will find a guide not just to achieving lofty valuations, but to navigating the realms of innovation, transformative leadership, and enduring success. It offers insights into the nuances of leadership, the forefront of emerging technologies, financial mastery, and the core of impactful entrepreneurship.

This series acknowledges the uniqueness of each entrepreneurial journey. Patrick delivers foundational wisdom alongside practical tools, emphasizing the tailored path each startup must navigate. Whether you're just beginning your entrepreneurial quest or are a seasoned professional fine-tuning your strategy, this book, and its series, light the way.

Step forward, challenge the status quo, and with "Unicorn Rising," ascend to unprecedented heights in your entrepreneurial venture.

Ignite Your Dream: The Quintessential Checklist for Aspiring Entrepreneurs
Ignite Your Dream: The Quintessential Checklist for Aspiring Entrepreneurs" by Patrick H. Perrine is an immersive guide lighting the path towards entrepreneurial success.

This power-packed handbook propels you from dreaming to achieving with a carefully curated 100-step map. Dive into real-life entrepreneur stories, extract wisdom, and utilize actionable checklists. This book transcends theoretical guidelines, providing a mentorship experience designed to turn dreams into reality.

Ready to kindle your entrepreneurial spirit? "Ignite your Dream" is your step forward towards unlocking potential and achieving success in the exciting world of entrepreneurship.

Fail Fast, Recover Faster: Bouncing Back From Entrepreneurial Failure

Embrace failure and bounce back stronger with "Fail Fast, Recover Faster: Bouncing Back From Entrepreneurial Failure". It's your guidebook through the tumultuous journey of entrepreneurship, celebrating stumbles as stepping stones towards success.

Dive into compelling tales of triumphant entrepreneurs, learn how to pivot rapidly, manage fallout, and convert setbacks into launchpads. Discover strategies for repairing financial, relationship, and reputation damage, and see your failures as badges of resilience.

This transformative book readies you to rebound from failure swiftly, turning your setbacks into your next entrepreneurial triumph. With "Fail Fast, Recover Faster", you're poised to harness your own unicorn moment and turn failure into a launching pad for success.

Fueling the Fire: Nurturing Resilience and Preventing Burnout in Entrepreneurship

In "Fueling the Fire: Nurturing Resilience and Preventing Burnout in Entrepreneurship," seasoned entrepreneur Patrick H. Perrine guides you through the entrepreneurial journey, sharing practical strategies for maintaining resilience and passion.

Drawing from 20 years of startup experience, Perrine covers everything from ideation to acquisition. Discover how to build a support system, manage your time effectively, cultivate a positive work culture, and align your work with your values.

Whether you're an experienced entrepreneur or just beginning, "Fueling the Fire" is a must-read for maintaining balance and fulfillment in the dynamic world of entrepreneurship.